MARRIAGE REMINDERS

Marriage Reminders

EXPLORE 15
CHRIST-CENTERED
MARRIAGE PRINCIPLES
TO REVIVE
AND STRENGTHEN YOUR
MARRIAGE.

Dr. Scott Reeder

Contents

1

Conflict Free Marriages Don't Exist

CONFLICT

"Let your conversation be always full of grace, seasoned with salt, so that you may know how to answer everyone" Colossians 4:6

CONFLICT FREE MARRIAGES DON'T EXIST

"If the two of you are going to fight this much, you don't need to get married." That was early advice from my now father-in-law of 37 years. You may not want to hear this from the marriage counselor and pastor, but the truth is, as far as couples go, my wife and I are fairly high on the conflict scale and always have been. I mean, if you were to check in with our now adult children, you would never hear them say, "I never saw my parents fight."

Negatively, we are stubborn, self-centered, and like to get our way. Positively, however, we care. See, conflict, in some measure, communicates care. When a spouse is willing to express and defend beliefs, opinions, and desires in marriage, it shows that they are invested in the marriage. The alternative is a spouse who is disengaged, apathetic, or simply does not care enough to engage. I am actually encouraged in marriage counseling when a couple in distress sits before me on intake, and as I ask them to express their feelings toward one another, she might say something like, "I am so angry at him," "I could choke him," "I don't even want to be around him right now." As a counselor, my thought is, "Great, she still cares about him enough to be angry with him."

Now, there is a right and a wrong way to do conflict. There is a healthy and unhealthy way to disagree, and a biblical and unbiblical approach to communication and conflict resolution. In our marriage, we have done well at this, and we have made a mess of it. It is only when we turn our hearts toward God that we seem to get it right. The Lord certainly has plenty to say about how we speak to each other and how we resolve our differences. We do well to look to the apostle Paul's letter to the Ephesian and Colossian churches. Here, just before Paul speaks to us about what a biblical marriage looks like, he reminds us how our identity in Christ should direct our actions, attitudes, and the way we speak to one another (see Ephesians 4:17-32; Colossians 3:1-17).

QUICK REMINDER

It is important to remember that every couple faces challenges in communication and conflict resolution. No marriage is immune to struggles.

Understanding that difficulties are a normal part of marriage can help normalize the issues couples face. While conflict is inevitable, couples should approach each other with patience, grace, and a willingness to learn and grow together. Show kindness, humility, empathy, and understanding, instead of allowing defensiveness, negativity, or bitterness to dominate your discussions.

GO DEEPER

While God's original design for marriage was one of unity, love, and harmony, sin entered the world and brought brokenness, including conflict, into human relationships. Conflict is not a bad thing, but it can be done in a bad way. Here are just some of the benefits of healthy conflict in marriage.

Refining and purifying: Just as fire purifies gold, conflicts in a marriage can refine and purify the relationship. In James 1:2-4, it is written, "Consider it pure joy, my brothers and sisters, whenever you face trials of many kinds, because you know that the testing of your faith produces perseverance." Through conflicts, couples have an opportunity to grow in patience, forgiveness, and understanding.

Communication and understanding: Conflict can reveal areas of disagreement or unmet expectations within a marriage. It provides an opportunity for open and honest communication, allowing both partners to express their thoughts, concerns, and desires. Ephesians 4:26-27 encourages resolving conflicts promptly and not letting anger fester, saying, "Do not let the sun go down while you are still angry."

Spiritual growth: Conflict in marriage can lead couples to rely on God's guidance and seek His wisdom in resolving their differences. It can foster humility, dependence on God, and a deepening of faith. Proverbs 3:5-6 reminds us to trust in the Lord and lean not on our understanding.

Strengthening unity: While conflicts can be challenging, overcoming them together can strengthen the bond between spouses. It requires humility, compromise, and the willingness to seek reconciliation. Romans 15:5 encourages believers to live in harmony with one another, striving for unity.

Reflecting Christ's love: In Ephesians 5:25, husbands are instructed to love their wives sacrificially, just as Christ loved the church. Conflict can provide an opportunity to demonstrate this sacrificial love, seeking the best interests of one another and working towards reconciliation.

However, it is essential to note that the Bible also emphasizes the importance of handling conflicts in a healthy and respectful manner. Ephesians 4:29-32 instructs believers to speak words that build up, to be kind and compassionate, and to forgive one another. Conflict should never be an excuse for abusive or harmful behavior within a marriage.

Ultimately, the goal is not to seek or avoid conflict, but rather to approach it as an opportunity for growth, understanding, and restoration within the marriage, relying on God's guidance and grace throughout the process.

QUESTIONS FOR REFLECTION

1. **How do we approach conflict in our marriage?**
   - Reflect on your typical responses to conflict. Do you avoid conflict, suppress your feelings, or engage in heated arguments?
   - Consider whether your approach promotes healthy communication, resolution, and growth within your relationship.
2. **How do we communicate during conflicts?**
   - Evaluate the effectiveness of your communication style during conflicts.
   - Do you actively listen to your spouse's perspective? Are you respectful and empathetic in your responses?
   - Reflect on how you can improve your communication to foster understanding and promote a peaceful resolution.
3. **How do we seek reconciliation after a conflict?**
   - Consider how you and your spouse work towards reconciliation following a conflict.
   - Do you apologize and seek forgiveness when necessary?
   - Do you make efforts to understand each other's perspectives and find common ground?
   - Reflect on the steps you can take to restore harmony and strengthen your relationship after conflicts arise.

Remember, these questions are meant to foster self-reflection and open dialogue with your spouse. Honest and open communication is crucial in addressing conflict in a healthy and constructive manner within your marriage.

TAKE ACTION

1. **Seek God's wisdom and guidance:**
   - Prioritize prayer and seek God's wisdom before addressing conflicts. Ask for His guidance in understanding the root causes of the conflict and in finding a resolution that aligns with His principles.
   - Study the Bible together to gain insights and wisdom on how to approach conflict resolution in a biblical manner.
   - Invite the Holy Spirit to work in your hearts, guiding your words and actions throughout the process.

2. **Embrace humility and a posture of reconciliation:**
   - Approach conflict with humility, acknowledging your own shortcomings and being open to correction.
   - Take responsibility for your part in the conflict and be willing to apologize and seek forgiveness when needed.
   - Foster a spirit of reconciliation by actively seeking to restore and strengthen the relationship, rather than winning an argument or proving yourself right.

3. **Engage in active listening and effective communication:**
   - Practice active listening by giving your full attention to your partner's perspective without interrupting or formulating responses.
   - Show empathy and seek to understand their feelings, needs, and concerns. Repeat back what you heard to ensure accurate understanding.
   - Communicate your thoughts and feelings in a respectful and loving manner, using "I" statements to express your perspective and avoid blame or criticism.

Remember, healthy biblical conflict resolution involves a willingness to prioritize the relationship, seek God's guidance, and engage in open and respectful communication. It is important to cultivate an atmosphere of love, grace, and reconciliation as you navigate conflicts within your marriage.

PRAYER FOR HELP

Heavenly Father, we come to You seeking Your guidance and wisdom in navigating conflicts within our marriage. Grant us patience, understanding, and a spirit of humility to approach disagreements with love and respect. Help us to communicate effectively, to listen attentively, and to find resolution that strengthens our bond and honors Your design for marriage. Amen.

2

Do Not Fall Into The Comparison Trap

COMPARISON

"I have learned to be content whatever the circumstances"
Philippians 4:11

DO NOT FALL INTO THE COMPARISON TRAP

Time is a good teacher. Early in our marriage, it was not uncommon to say things like, "If you would just treat me like he treats his wife," or "Do you see the way she supports her husband?" Not to make light of having other marriages we can look toward as good examples in our marriage, but we learned quickly that there were no such things as perfect examples. The truth is many of the couples and spouses we pointed to, at some point or another, showed their true imperfect selves.

People tend to put out and display their best selves. Behind closed doors, however, the reality that we all married imperfect sinners is made perfectly clear. Over the years, we learned to pay less attention to what others have or appeared to have and spend more time reflecting on how God has abundantly blessed us beyond what we deserve (see 2 Corinthians 9:8; Philippians 4:11-12). Now, instead of comparing ourselves to other couples, we seek the Lord to help us better steward all He has gifted us with in our own marriage and family.

We still find ourselves desiring what others have. The funny thing is, though, the couples we now desire to imitate are the ones who, with God's grace, are authentically doing their best to grow in Christlikeness toward others and toward each other (see 2 Corinthians 3:18; Philippians 1:6).

QUICK REMINDER

Understand that every marriage is unique, with its own dynamics, strengths, and challenges. In marriage, it's easy to fall into the trap of comparing our relationship to others. We may see what others have and feel dissatisfied with our own circumstances. Instead of constantly longing for what others have, we can focus on the unique joys and strengths in our relationship.

Avoid comparing your marriage to others or idealized notions of what a perfect marriage should be like. Perfect (people) marriages don't exist. Acknowledge that no marriage is perfect, and then set realistic expectations for your marriage, recognizing that it will have its highs and lows.

GO DEEPER

In the Bible, comparing oneself to others is generally discouraged as it can lead to envy, discontentment, and division. This principle applies to various aspects of life, including marriage. When couples start comparing themselves to other couples, it can negatively impact their relationship in several ways. Here are some biblical insights to consider:

Contentment and gratitude: The Bible encourages believers to cultivate an attitude of contentment and gratitude. Philippians 4:11-12 states, "I have learned to be content whatever the circumstances. I know what it is to be in need, and I know what it is to have plenty." Instead of comparing your marriage to others, focus on appreciating the blessings and unique qualities of your own relationship. Gratitude helps foster a healthier perspective and promotes marital satisfaction.

Individuality and uniqueness: Each marriage is unique, with its own strengths, challenges, and dynamics. Comparing your marriage to others disregards the individuality and uniqueness that God has designed for your relationship. Romans 12:6 reminds believers that "we have different gifts, according to the grace given to each of us." Embrace the distinctive qualities and dynamics of your own marriage, recognizing that God has a purpose for your relationship that may differ from others.

Trusting God's plan: Trusting in God's plan and timing is essential in marriage. Comparison can stem from a lack of trust in God's provision and His unique path for your relationship. Proverbs 3:5-6 advises, "Trust in the LORD with all your heart and lean not on your own understanding; in all your ways submit to him, and he will make your paths straight." Instead of comparing, seek God's guidance and trust in His plan for your marriage. He knows what is best for you and your spouse.

It is important for couples to focus on nurturing and cultivating their own relationship, rather than measuring themselves against others. Embrace the strengths, challenges, and growth opportunities within your marriage, and remember that God's love and grace are sufficient for your journey together.

QUESTIONS FOR REFLECTION

1. **What triggers feelings of comparison in our marriage?**
   - Reflect on the specific situations, circumstances, or aspects that tend to lead you or your spouse into comparing your marriage to others.
   - Is it related to material possessions, career success, appearance, or other areas? Identifying these triggers can help you address them more effectively.

2. **How does comparison affect our relationship?**
   - Consider the impact that comparison has on your marriage. Does it breed discontentment, resentment, or dissatisfaction? Does it create unnecessary pressure or unrealistic expectations?
   - Reflect on the ways in which comparison hinders the growth, intimacy, and joy within your relationship.

3. **How can we cultivate contentment and gratitude in our marriage?**
   - Shift the focus from comparing to cultivating contentment and gratitude.
   - Reflect on the blessings, strengths, and growth opportunities within your own marriage.
   - Discuss ways in which you can foster an atmosphere of gratitude and appreciation for one another.
   - How can you celebrate and embrace the unique qualities and dynamics of your relationship?

Remember, the goal is to shift your perspective away from comparison and towards gratitude, contentment, and embracing the journey that God has designed for your marriage. Honest and open communication with your spouse is key to addressing comparison and nurturing a healthy, fulfilling relationship together.

TAKE ACTION

1. **Cultivate gratitude and contentment:**
   - Regularly practice gratitude by intentionally focusing on the blessings and positive aspects of your own marriage. Count your blessings and express gratitude to God and your spouse for what you have.
   - Develop a mindset of contentment by recognizing that God has uniquely designed your marriage for His purposes. Trust in His plan and timing for your relationship, appreciating the unique qualities and dynamics that make your marriage special.
2. **Renew your mind with biblical truths:**
   - Fill your mind with biblical truths about identity, worth, and the purpose of marriage. Study passages such as Psalm 139:14, which affirms that you and your spouse are fearfully and wonderfully made by God.
   - Meditate on verses that emphasize God's love, grace, and faithfulness in your marriage. For example, Ephesians 5:25 reminds husbands to love their wives sacrificially, just as Christ loved the church.
3. **Focus on personal growth and stewardship:**
   - Instead of comparing yourself to other couples, prioritize personal growth and stewardship of your own marriage. Invest time and effort into developing a strong and loving relationship with your spouse.
   - Seek ways to improve communication, deepen intimacy, and strengthen your commitment to one another.

○ Pursue opportunities for personal and marital growth, such as attending marriage seminars, reading books on healthy relationships, or seeking mentorship from a wise and mature couple.

By cultivating gratitude, renewing your mind with biblical truths, and focusing on personal growth and stewardship, you can shift your perspective away from comparison and towards embracing the unique blessings and purpose God has for your marriage. Remember, comparison steals joy and contentment, but God desires for you to experience His abundant love and fulfillment within your own relationship.

PRAYER FOR HELP

Loving Father, we surrender our hearts to You, asking for Your guidance in our marriage. Protect us from the snare of comparison, reminding us that each couple's journey is unique and ordained by You. Help us focus on the blessings, strengths, and growth in our own relationship, and grant us contentment and gratitude for the love we share. Amen.

3

We Are All Different - And That's OK

PERSONALITY

"There are different kinds of gifts, but the same Spirit distributes them. There are different kinds of service, but the same Lord. There are different kinds of working, but in all of them and in everyone it is the same God at work." 1 Corinthians 12:4-6

WE ARE ALL DIFFERENT - AND THAT'S OK

I promise you, morning people are not more spiritual. Lisa is up at 5 a.m., ready to tackle the world, and also ready to yank me from the clutches of sweet slumber in order to discuss the day's activities. I am barely rolling over, and I will need to hit snooze several more times before I allow my first cup of coffee and the morning sun to bring me back to life. I likely stayed up until at least midnight and often several hours later. During that time, I was ready to discuss the day, productively plan the next, and just get things done before bed. When I tried my best to engage her in deep conversation, she likely replied, 'I'm done for the day, I'm already in bed, I just haven't made it there yet.'

As a marriage counselor, I have administered and surveyed hundreds of personality profiles and have helped couples navigate their differences and similarities (yes, similarities can be a struggle as well). The issue is often this: we most want someone to be like us, and if they are not like us, we have decided that who we are is 'good' and who they are is 'bad.' So, I titled this particular couples counseling session on personality, 'Not Good - Not Bad - Just Different.'

Interestingly enough, I always start the session by reading from 1 Corinthians 12, where the Apostle Paul discusses at length the various gifts God has given individuals in the church. Gifts that, when brought together in unity, have the ability to make a stronger whole within the body of Christ. Well, in the same way that diversity does not guarantee unity in the church, it is not a guarantee in marriage either. We must seek God's help not only to accept each other but to leverage our differences to make a better whole. Unity in diversity—that is God's plan, not to make us all the same.

QUICK REMINDER

Do birds of a feather flock together or do opposites attract? Every individual has a unique personality, and God has created us differently. In marriage, we must navigate both our similarities and differences to build a strong relationship. Doing so requires negotiation, understanding, and a willingness to embrace each other's individuality. Cultivate a relationship built on mutual respect and equality.

GO DEEPER

In a marriage, it is not solely about being completely alike or always agreeing on everything. Rather, the focus should be on cultivating mutual respect and recognizing the equality of both partners before God. It involves honoring each other's perspectives, embracing differences, and valuing the worth and dignity of both individuals in the marriage relationship.

The Bible affirms the value of diversity of personality within a marriage, recognizing that God has uniquely designed individuals with distinct personalities, strengths, and gifts. Here are some biblical insights on the value of diversity of personality in a marriage:

Complementarity and Unity: In Genesis 1:27, it is written that God created humankind in His own image, male and female He created them. Men and women, with their unique personalities and qualities, are designed to complement one another in marriage. Their diverse strengths and perspectives contribute to a greater unity and wholeness as they work together as a team.

Body of Christ analogy: The apostle Paul uses the analogy of the body in 1 Corinthians 12:12-27 to describe the unity and interdependence of believers within the Church. Just as the different parts of the body have distinct functions and roles, individuals within a marriage bring their unique personalities and strengths to contribute to the overall health and functioning of the relationship.

Growth and Learning Opportunities: In a diverse personality dynamic, couples have opportunities to grow and learn from one another. Proverbs 27:17 states, "As iron sharpens iron, so one person sharpens another." The differences in personality can challenge each spouse to develop patience, understanding, and appreciation for one another's unique qualities. They can learn to navigate and appreciate different communication styles, problem-solving approaches, and perspectives, which leads to personal growth and mutual understanding.

Embracing diversity of personality in a marriage allows spouses to celebrate and leverage their unique strengths, supporting and complementing one another in different aspects of life. It fosters mutual respect, growth, and unity as they navigate the challenges and joys of life together. It is important to remember that diversity should be embraced within the context of love, respect, and the pursuit of unity in Christ.

QUESTIONS FOR REFLECTION

1. **How does our diversity of personality enhance our relationship?**
    - Reflect on the specific ways in which your unique personalities complement and enhance one another.
    - Consider the strengths, talents, and perspectives that each of you brings to the marriage.

- How do these differences contribute to a more balanced and fulfilling partnership?

2. **How can we appreciate and value each other's differences?**
   - Consider how you currently appreciate and value each other's diverse personalities.
   - Are there areas where you can grow in embracing and celebrating these differences even more?
   - Reflect on the importance of showing respect, understanding, and acceptance for your spouse's unique qualities and ways of being.

3. **How can we leverage our diversity of personality for growth and unity?**
   - Explore how your diverse personalities can be harnessed for personal and relational growth.
   - Discuss ways in which you can learn from one another, leveraging your differences to develop new skills, broaden perspectives, and deepen your understanding of each other and the world around you.
   - How can you use your unique qualities to strengthen the unity and bond in your marriage?

Remember, these questions are meant to foster self-reflection and open dialogue with your spouse. Embrace the diversity of personality within your marriage as an opportunity for growth, learning, and mutual appreciation. By understanding and valuing each other's differences, you can create a richer and more fulfilling relationship together.

TAKE ACTION

1. **Practice empathy and understanding:**
   - Make a conscious effort to understand and empathize with your spouse's perspective, even if it differs from your own.

○ Seek to see things from their point of view and validate their feelings and experiences.

○ Cultivate a heart of compassion and patience, recognizing that your spouse's unique personality traits and preferences have their own value and significance.

2. **Communicate with openness and respect:**

○ Foster open and respectful communication in your marriage.

○ Create a safe space where both of you can freely express your thoughts, feelings, and needs without fear of judgment or criticism.

○ Listen attentively to your spouse's ideas and opinions, even if they differ from yours. Engage in active dialogue, seeking to understand and learn from each other's perspectives.

3. **Celebrate and leverage each other's strengths:**

○ Recognize and celebrate the unique strengths and qualities that each of you brings to the marriage.

○ Appreciate the ways in which your diverse personalities complement and enhance one another.

○ Seek opportunities to leverage each other's strengths and talents.

○ Encourage and support your spouse in pursuing their passions and using their unique gifts to contribute to the marriage and the world around you.

By practicing empathy, fostering open communication, and celebrating each other's strengths, you can biblically encourage the embracing of diversity of personality in your marriage. Remember, God has created both of you with unique qualities for a purpose, and by embracing and valuing these differences, you can strengthen your relationship and grow together in love and unity.

PRAYER FOR HELP

Gracious Lord, we lift our voices in gratitude for the beautiful diversity You have woven into our marriage. Help us embrace and celebrate the unique personalities, strengths, and perspectives You have bestowed upon us. Grant us the wisdom and love to appreciate and learn from one another, growing together in unity while cherishing the beautiful diversity that reflects Your creativity and wisdom. Amen.

4

Forgiveness Is Key

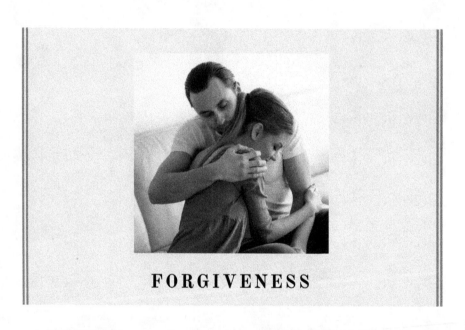

FORGIVENESS

"Be kind and compassionate to one another, forgiving each other, just as in Christ God forgave you." Ephesians 4:32

FORGIVENESS IS KEY

I like to begin my premarital counseling with this question: 'In a word, what do you think it will take to make your marriage work?' There are always some great responses. Of course, 'God' or 'Christ' are the most accurate answers. Yet, I often hear people say things like trust, communication, love, respect, honesty, patience, and sacrifice. I acknowledge that all of these are good answers. But the one I often do not hear, and the one I believe is the key to a lasting marriage, is forgiveness. You see, we all marry flawed individuals in need of God's forgiveness, and we are often reminded that we are to forgive as the Lord forgives (Ephesians 4:32).

The alternative is unforgiveness, bitterness, revenge, holding grudges, and allowing the enemy to further embitter us toward each other. I do believe a prerequisite to transactional forgiveness requires confession and repentance (see Luke 17:3-4). But before transactional forgiveness, comes attitudinal forgiveness, which is marked by a ready heart of forgiveness that seeks to extend grace even in the face of clear wrongdoing (see Matthew 6:14-15).

A strong marriage is a forgiving marriage. Forgiveness is not forgetting, it does not remove consequences, and it does not automatically restore trust. What it does is open the door to reconciliation, and a strong marriage understands that reconciliation is needed because conflicts and misunderstandings will arise throughout the course of a marriage. If the Lord can bear with and forgive us, how could we not treat each other in like manner (see Colossians 3:13)?

QUICK REMINDER

Recognize that both of you will at times will hurt, betray, and let each other down. You will make mistakes and therefore you must be willing to forgive and seek forgiveness. Practicing forgiveness allows us to let go of past hurts, promotes healing, and creates space for growth and reconciliation in our marriages.

According to the Bible, forgiveness plays a vital role in maintaining a healthy marriage relationship. Scripture teaches that God is a forgiving God who extends grace and mercy to His people.

GO DEEPER

God's forgiveness and example: In Ephesians 4:32, believers are encouraged to "be kind to one another, tenderhearted, forgiving one another, as God in Christ forgave you." Just as God forgives our sins and shortcomings through Christ's sacrifice, we are called to extend that forgiveness to our spouse.

Love and reconciliation: The foundation of a healthy marriage is love. 1 Peter 4:8 states, "Above all, love each other deeply, because love covers over a multitude of sins." Forgiveness is an expression of love and an essential component of reconciliation. It allows for healing, restoration, and the rebuilding of trust in the relationship.

The Lord's Prayer: In the Lord's Prayer found in Matthew 6:12, Jesus instructs his disciples to pray, "And forgive us our debts, as we also have forgiven our debtors." This prayer reminds us of the importance of both seeking and extending forgiveness. When we forgive our spouse, we align ourselves with the heart of God and invite His grace and healing into our marriage.

Forgiveness in marriage involves letting go of resentment, bitterness, and the desire for revenge. It is an ongoing process that requires humility, empathy, and a willingness to reconcile. Forgiveness does not ignore or condone wrongdoing, but it releases the burden of anger and resentment, fostering an environment of grace, healing, and growth.

By embracing forgiveness in your marriage, you create space for God's love and restoration to flourish. It allows you and your spouse to move forward, strengthen your bond, and experience the fullness of God's grace in your relationship. Remember, forgiveness is not always easy, but it is a powerful and transformative act that reflects God's character and brings healing and restoration to your marriage.

QUESTIONS FOR REFLECTION

1. **Am I holding onto any unforgiveness or resentment towards my spouse?**
   - Reflect on your heart and examine whether there are any unresolved issues, hurts, or grievances that you are holding onto. Are there any areas where you have not fully forgiven your spouse? Are there lingering feelings of resentment or bitterness?
   - Consider how holding onto unforgiveness may be affecting your emotional well-being, your relationship with your spouse, and your overall marital satisfaction.
2. **How can I extend forgiveness and grace to my spouse?**
   - Reflect on the specific areas where your spouse may have hurt or wronged you. Are you willing to extend

forgiveness and grace to them? Are there any specific actions or behaviors that you need to forgive and release?

- Consider the biblical example of forgiveness and the sacrificial love of Christ. How can you embody that forgiveness and extend grace to your spouse, allowing for healing and reconciliation in your marriage?

3. **What steps can we take to foster a culture of forgiveness in our marriage?**

- Reflect on the overall atmosphere of forgiveness in your marriage. Are there any patterns of unforgiveness or conflict that need to be addressed and transformed? How can you cultivate an environment of grace, understanding, and forgiveness?

- Discuss practical steps that you and your spouse can take to foster a culture of forgiveness, such as open and honest communication, seeking reconciliation, practicing empathy, and committing to ongoing forgiveness and growth.

Remember, forgiveness is a journey that requires intentionality and a commitment to healing and reconciliation. These questions are meant to foster self-reflection and open dialogue with your spouse. By addressing forgiveness within your marriage, you can experience greater emotional well-being, deeper intimacy, and a stronger foundation for a healthy and thriving relationship.

TAKE ACTION

1. **Cultivate a heart of humility and grace:**

- Recognize your own need for forgiveness and the grace that God has extended to you. Develop a humble and compassionate attitude towards your spouse, acknowledging that both of you are imperfect and in need of forgiveness.

- Practice self-reflection and repentance, acknowledging your own shortcomings and seeking God's forgiveness. This will help foster a spirit of humility and grace in your marriage.

2. **Foster open and honest communication:**

- Create a safe and non-judgmental space for open and honest communication in your marriage. Encourage your spouse to express their thoughts, feelings, and concerns without fear of condemnation.
- Initiate conversations about forgiveness when necessary. Discuss past hurts, conflicts, and areas of unforgiveness, seeking to understand each other's perspectives and working towards reconciliation.

3. **Remember, forgiveness will take time and effort:**

- Embrace biblical principles of forgiveness and reconciliation in your marriage. Follow Jesus' teaching in Matthew 18:21-22 to forgive "not seven times, but seventy-seven times." Cultivate a heart of forgiveness that is willing to extend grace and let go of past hurts.
- Seek reconciliation and restoration in your relationship. When conflicts arise, approach them with a spirit of humility, seeking resolution rather than winning an argument. Be willing to apologize, seek forgiveness, and offer forgiveness to your spouse.

4. **Practice the principles of forgiveness and reconciliation:**

- By cultivating a heart of humility and grace, fostering open communication, and practicing the principles of forgiveness and reconciliation, you can encourage a culture of forgiveness in your marriage. Through God's grace and guidance, forgiveness can bring healing, restoration, and greater intimacy in your relationship.

PRAYER FOR HELP

Merciful Father, we humbly come before You, acknowledging our need for Your divine grace and forgiveness. Help us to fully embrace and extend forgiveness within our marriage, releasing any resentment or bitterness that may hinder our relationship. Grant us the strength to apologize, seek reconciliation, and offer genuine forgiveness, following the example of Your unconditional love and forgiveness towards us. Amen.

5

Build A Thankful Marriage

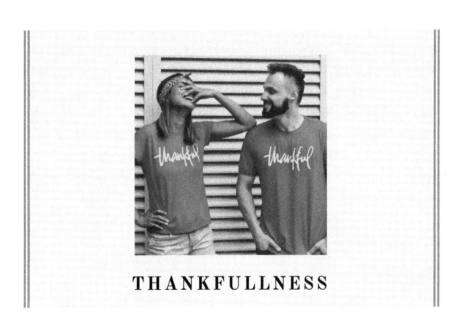

THANKFULLNESS

"Give thanks in all circumstances; for this is God's will for you in Christ Jesus." 1 Thessalonians 5:18

BUILD A THANKFUL MARRIAGE

Not a day goes by that you cannot thank your spouse for something. Each day, there are a myriad of things that Lisa and I do in order to serve each other. Many of these things are just about being a supportive marriage partner, getting done what needs to be done, and taking care of the family. The things we do for each other do not "require" a thank you. But when that simple, appreciative, unnecessary gesture comes, it often puts wind in the sails of the recipient. It says, 'I saw that, I was blessed by that, I am thankful for you.' A simple thank you expresses a truly appreciative heart toward one another in marriage.

So the next time your spouse drops something off, picks something up, cooks a great meal, trims the shrubs, gets up early, stays up late, comes home early, or works overtime to provide, why not slow down to deliver a simple 'Thank You, I Really Appreciate _____.' You might get an 'oh, don't mention it' or 'no problem,' but what you have really done is made a deposit of some equity into the love bank of your spouse's heart. This is relational equity you might need to spend on a day when you really make a mess of it. Trust me, I say unnecessary thank you's a lot!

QUICK REMINDER

By regularly expressing appreciation for our spouse and the blessings within our relationship, we cultivate a positive and nurturing environment. Gratitude helps us focus on the good, strengthens emotional bonds, and fosters a sense of contentment and satisfaction. It promotes mutual respect, encourages acts of kindness, and enhances overall marital satisfaction. Embracing gratitude in marriage brings about greater happiness and strengthens the foundation of the relationship.

GO DEEPER

According to the Bible, thankfulness is indeed vital to a happy marriage relationship. Here are some biblical insights that highlight the importance of thankfulness:

Gratitude as an Attitude: In numerous passages, the Bible encourages believers to have an attitude of gratitude. 1 Thessalonians 5:18 states, "Give thanks in all circumstances; for this is the will of God in Christ Jesus for you." Thankfulness is not dependent on circumstances but is a choice to acknowledge and appreciate the blessings and goodness of God.

Cultivating Contentment: Thankfulness fosters contentment and prevents the tendency to take one another for granted. Philippians 4:11-12 says, "I have learned to be content whatever the circumstances...I have learned the secret of being content in any and every situation." Expressing gratitude for each other and the gifts God has bestowed helps maintain a sense of satisfaction and joy in the marriage.

Strengthening the Bond: Thankfulness and appreciation in marriage strengthen the bond between spouses. Proverbs 15:23 says, "A person finds joy in giving an apt reply—and how good is a timely word!" Expressing gratitude towards one another uplifts the spirit, encourages the heart, and deepens the sense of love and connection within the relationship.

Practicing thankfulness in a marriage involves consciously acknowledging and expressing gratitude for the qualities, actions, and efforts of your spouse. It involves recognizing and appreciating the blessings of God's grace in your lives and the ways in which your spouse contributes to your happiness and well-being.

By cultivating a heart of thankfulness, you nurture an atmosphere of appreciation and love in your marriage. Regularly expressing gratitude and thanksgiving towards your spouse strengthens the bond, fosters a positive outlook, and creates a foundation of joy and contentment. Remember, gratitude is not only a beneficial practice for your marriage but also a reflection of your faith and trust in God's provision and goodness.

QUESTIONS FOR REFLECTION

1. **What are three specific qualities or actions of my spouse that I am grateful for?**
   - Reflect on the unique qualities, actions, or gestures that your spouse possesses or does that you genuinely appreciate.
   - Consider how they contribute to your happiness, growth, and the well-being of your marriage.

2. **In what ways can I express my gratitude and thankfulness to my spouse?**
   - Consider the various ways in which you can express your thankfulness to your spouse.
   - Reflect on specific actions, words, or gestures that would effectively communicate your appreciation.
   - Think about their love language and how you can tailor your expressions of gratitude to resonate with them.

3. **How can we cultivate a culture of thankfulness in our marriage?**
   - Explore ways in which you and your spouse can intentionally foster a culture of thankfulness in your marriage.
   - Reflect on habits, routines, or rituals that you can implement to regularly express gratitude to one another.

○ Discuss how you can encourage and remind each other to be thankful for the blessings and gifts in your lives.

Remember, expressing thankfulness is not a one-time event but an ongoing practice. These questions are meant to inspire self-reflection and open dialogue with your spouse. By intentionally reflecting on and expressing gratitude, you can strengthen your marital bond, cultivate joy and contentment, and create an atmosphere of love and appreciation in your marriage.

TAKE ACTION:

1. **Cultivate a heart of gratitude:**
   ○ Develop a personal habit of gratitude by intentionally focusing on the positive aspects of your spouse and your marriage. Regularly reflect on the blessings and qualities that you appreciate in your spouse.
   ○ Practice gratitude towards God as well, recognizing that your spouse is a gift from Him. Cultivating a heart of gratitude towards God will naturally overflow into gratitude for your spouse.
2. **Express thankfulness directly and regularly:**
   ○ Make it a practice to express your gratitude and appreciation to your spouse directly and regularly. Take the time to sincerely thank them for specific actions, qualities, or gestures that you appreciate.
   ○ Use both words and actions to convey your thankfulness. Write a heartfelt note, prepare a thoughtful surprise, or simply verbalize your gratitude in everyday conversations.
3. **Create rituals of thankfulness:**
   ○ Establish rituals or traditions within your marriage that promote thankfulness. For example, you can start or end

each day by sharing something you are grateful for about your spouse.

○ Consider incorporating prayer into your gratitude rituals. Take time to thank God together for the gift of your spouse and express gratitude for the ways they contribute to your life.

By cultivating a heart of gratitude, expressing thankfulness directly and regularly, and creating rituals of thankfulness, you can encourage and nurture a culture of gratitude in your marriage. Remember, expressing gratitude not only blesses your spouse but also enhances your own perspective, fostering a deeper appreciation for the gift of your marriage. Let thankfulness become a foundational aspect of your relationship, rooted in your faith and love for one another.

PRAYER FOR HELP

Gracious Father, we humbly come before You, grateful for the gift of our spouse. Please help us to cultivate hearts of gratitude and appreciation for them, recognizing the unique qualities and blessings they bring to our marriage. Grant us the words, actions, and opportunities to express our thankfulness to our spouse, and may our love and gratitude reflect Your love and grace in our relationship. Amen.

6

Nurture Emotional And Physical Intimacy

INTIMACY

"I belong to my beloved, and his desire is for me." Song of Solomon 7:10

NURTURE EMOTIONAL AND PHYSICAL INTIMACY

God is not ashamed of sex. He created it. I can think of at least three purposes for physical sexual intimacy: procreation, pleasure, and to bring glory to the Creator. Yes, sex was given as a reproductive act that has served well since the foundation of creation. Next, God gave us sex as a great source of pleasure to be enjoyed within the parameters and intentions of the gift. There are a whole lot of nerve endings in very specific places that deliver very intentional brain signals when aroused. None of that is a biological accident; it is a very intentional design from a very intentional God.

Sex is not all of a marriage, but it is to be enjoyed as one of God's good gifts in marriage. It is important to note that the Bible also emphasizes the sanctity and exclusivity of sexual intimacy within marriage. 1 Corinthians 7:2-5 teaches that sexual intimacy is a vital part of marriage. This physical aspect of intimacy should be nurtured within the context of emotional intimacy, trust, and mutual consent.

These passages further state that husbands and wives have a responsibility to fulfill each other's sexual needs. The passage highlights the mutual authority and submission in this aspect of the marital relationship, urging spouses not to withhold themselves from one another except by mutual agreement. It also underscores the importance of sexual intimacy in guarding against temptation and maintaining self-control.

QUICK REMINDER

Nurturing emotional and physical intimacy is crucial for a healthy marriage. Spouse are encouraged to find joy and fulfillment in each other, as this emphasizes the unique and sacred bond of marriage. Make time for quality conversations, shared activities, and expressions of love and affection. Be attentive to each other's emotional needs and work together to maintain a fulfilling intimate life.

In the Bible, emotional and physical intimacy in marriage are interconnected and designed to complement one another within the context of a committed, marital relationship.

GO DEEPER

Unity and Oneness: Genesis 2:24 describes God's intention for marriage, saying, "Therefore a man shall leave his father and his mother and hold fast to his wife, and they shall become one flesh." This unity encompasses not only physical union but also emotional, spiritual, and relational unity. Emotional intimacy strengthens the bond between spouses and enhances their physical connection.

Selfless Love and Intimacy: The Bible teaches that love within marriage should be selfless and sacrificial. Ephesians 5:25 states, "Husbands, love your wives, as Christ loved the church and gave himself up for her." This selfless love fosters emotional intimacy as spouses prioritize the well-being, needs, and emotions of one another. Emotional intimacy, in turn, enhances physical intimacy by creating an environment of trust, vulnerability, and deep connection.

Intimacy as a Reflection of God's Love: The Song of Solomon portrays the beauty and passion of marital love, celebrating both emotional and physical intimacy. This book demonstrates how emotional and physical expressions of love in marriage are a reflection of God's design and his intention for marital fulfillment.

Emotional and physical intimacy in marriage are intertwined and mutually beneficial. Emotional intimacy strengthens the connection between spouses, fostering trust, vulnerability, and selfless love. This, in turn, enhances physical intimacy, which is designed to be a beautiful and fulfilling expression of love within the boundaries of a marital relationship.

QUESTIONS FOR REFLECTION

1. **How do we nurture emotional intimacy in our marriage?**
   - Reflect on the quality of emotional connection and communication within your marriage. Do you feel understood, valued, and emotionally supported by your spouse? Are you actively investing in deepening your emotional bond?
   - Consider the ways you can enhance emotional intimacy, such as through open and honest communication, active listening, sharing thoughts and feelings, and prioritizing quality time together.
2. **How do we cultivate and prioritize physical intimacy in our marriage?**
   - Reflect on the state of your physical intimacy. Are you both satisfied with the level of physical affection, romance, and sexual intimacy in your relationship? Do you prioritize and invest in this aspect of your marriage?
   - Consider any barriers or challenges that may hinder physical intimacy and explore ways to address them, whether

through open communication, seeking professional help if needed, or exploring new ways to enhance your physical connection.

3. **Are there any past wounds or unresolved issues that hinder our intimacy?**

   ○ Reflect on any past hurts, unresolved conflicts, or emotional wounds that may be affecting your intimacy. Are there any underlying issues that need to be addressed and healed?

   ○ Consider seeking professional help or counseling if necessary to navigate and heal from any past wounds, allowing for greater emotional and physical intimacy to flourish in your marriage.

Remember, these questions are meant to foster self-reflection and open dialogue with your spouse. Honest and open communication is crucial in nurturing intimacy in your marriage. By addressing these questions and actively working towards deepening emotional and physical intimacy, you can strengthen the bond and connection with your spouse.

TAKE ACTION

1. **Cultivate a foundation of love, respect, and selflessness:**

   ○ Embrace the biblical principle of love and selflessness in your marriage. Follow the example of Christ's sacrificial love for the church (Ephesians 5:25) by actively demonstrating love, kindness, and respect towards your spouse.

   ○ Prioritize your spouse's emotional and physical well-being above your own. Serve and support them selflessly, seeking to meet their needs and desires.

2. **Foster open and honest communication:**

- Create a safe and non-judgmental space for open and honest communication. Encourage your spouse to freely express their thoughts, emotions, desires, and concerns.
- Practice active listening, seeking to understand your spouse's perspective without interrupting or being defensive. Validate their feelings and respond with empathy and compassion.
- Communicate your own needs, desires, and boundaries to your spouse, allowing for mutual understanding and growth.

3. **Prioritize intentional time for emotional and physical connection:**
   - Set aside dedicated time for emotional and physical intimacy in your marriage. Make it a priority to spend quality time together, engaging in activities that foster emotional connection and intimacy.
   - Create a loving and romantic atmosphere within your home. Prioritize physical affection, such as hugging, kissing, and holding hands, to foster a sense of closeness and connection.
   - Be intentional about nurturing your sexual intimacy within the boundaries of your marriage, respecting and honoring one another's needs and desires.

Remember to seek God's guidance and wisdom in nurturing emotional and physical intimacy. Regularly pray for your marriage and seek opportunities to grow together spiritually. By cultivating love, fostering open communication, and prioritizing intentional time for connection, you can encourage emotional and physical intimacy in a way that aligns with biblical principles.

PRAYER FOR HELP

Loving Father, we seek Your guidance and blessing as we strive to cultivate emotional and physical intimacy within our marriage. Grant us open hearts and vulnerability to share our deepest thoughts, feelings, and desires with one another. Strengthen the bond of love between us, allowing emotional and physical intimacy to flourish, reflecting Your design for marital union. Amen

7

Prioritize Couple Time Together

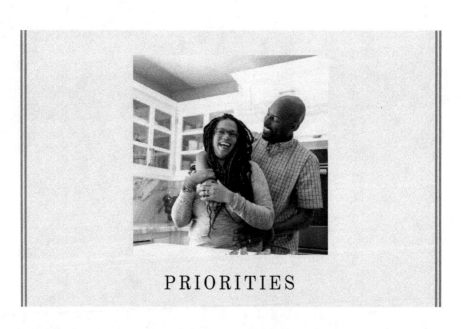

PRIORITIES

"For this reason, a man will leave his father and mother and be united to his wife, and the two will become one flesh. So they are no longer two, but one flesh. Therefore what God has joined together, let no one separate."
Matthew 19:5-6

PRIORITIZE COUPLE TIME TOGETHER

Confession - I don't care for yard sales. In fact, Lisa would never ask me on a Friday evening, 'What do you want to do tomorrow?' and hear me reply, 'Why don't we go to some yard sales?' At the same time, I am pretty sure she does not enjoy going to Home Depot or NASCAR races. Now, there are many things we both enjoy doing together, but occasionally, together, we go to yard sales, and she goes with me to the hardware store or a car race. Why? Because more than what we are doing, we enjoy who we are doing it with.

We fully understand and appreciate the need to have some guy friends and some girl friends, and we have engaged in couples' small groups for many, many years. Those relationships encourage us, support us, hold us accountable, and ultimately make me a better husband and father, and her a better wife and mother. These relationships also make us both better Christ-followers. In addition to those relationships, we simply love to hang out with our children, and as of this writing, our nine grandchildren. But we also spend a lot of time together, just me and her. We understand the value of prioritizing our time together so we don't drift into living as strangers in our marriage.

Finally, we love to occasionally go big - a flight to a new adventure, a cruise destination, a marriage conference, a weekend away. But we also value a quiet walk, attending worship together, cooking a meal, sitting by the pool, or just watching a movie together." We understand that 'quality time' is found in 'quantity time.'

QUICK REMINDER

The Bible encourages couples to prioritize spending time together as a means of strengthening their marriage, deepening their emotional connection, and fostering intimacy. By intentionally setting aside time for one another, couples honor the sacred bond of marriage and create a foundation for a thriving and fulfilling relationship.

By prioritizing one another and spending intentional time together, couples honor the sacredness of their union, demonstrate selfless love, and create an environment where their marriage can thrive.

GO DEEPER

The Bible highlights the significance of prioritizing each other and spending time together in marriage through various passages:

The Primary Relationship: Matthew 19:5-6: Jesus affirms the importance of the marital bond, stating, "For this reason, a man will leave his father and mother and be united to his wife, and the two will become one flesh... Therefore what God has joined together, let no one separate." Prioritizing one another means recognizing and honoring the special union that God has created, placing each other above all other earthly relationships.

Sacrificial Love: Ephesians 5:25: The apostle Paul instructs husbands to love their wives sacrificially, just as Christ loved the church. Prioritizing one another involves selflessness and a willingness to invest time and effort into nurturing the relationship. It means considering the needs and desires of your spouse, seeking to build them up and show them love in practical ways.

Deepening the Bond: In Genesis 2:24, God establishes marriage as a sacred union, declaring that a man and woman become "one flesh." By spending quality time together, couples nurture their emotional connection, deepen their understanding of one another, and strengthen the bond of unity that God intended for marriage.

Delighting in each other: Ecclesiastes 9:9: The book of Ecclesiastes encourages enjoying the blessings of life, including the companionship of one's spouse. It says, "Enjoy life with your wife, whom you love, all the days of this meaningless life that God has given you under the sun —all your meaningless days. For this is your lot in life and in your toilsome labor under the sun." Prioritizing time together involves actively cherishing and delighting in the companionship and love shared with your spouse.

Investing time in each other nurtures emotional connection, fosters communication, and allows for the growth of love, unity, and mutual support. Ultimately, prioritizing one another reflects God's design for marriage and contributes to the fulfillment and joy found in the marital relationship.

QUESTIONS FOR REFLECTION:

1. **How am I currently prioritizing my spouse in our relationship?**
   - Reflect on your daily routines, activities, and decisions to assess whether your spouse is a priority in your life.
   - Consider how you allocate your time, energy, and resources, and honestly evaluate whether your spouse feels valued and prioritized.

2. **What changes or adjustments can I make to better prioritize my spouse?**
   - Identify areas where you can improve in prioritizing your spouse. Are there commitments, distractions, or habits that need to be reassessed?
   - Consider practical steps you can take to invest more time, attention, and effort into your relationship, ensuring that your spouse feels cherished and prioritized.

3. **How can we create intentional time together and strengthen our bond?**
   - Explore ways to carve out dedicated quality time for one another.
   - Discuss together how you can create regular routines, rituals, or activities that allow for meaningful connection and emotional intimacy.
   - Brainstorm ideas for shared interests, date nights, or focused conversations that can strengthen your bond and foster a deeper sense of priority and love.

By honestly reflecting on these questions, you can gain insights into your current dynamics and take proactive steps to prioritize your spouse in your marriage. Remember, prioritizing each other requires intentionality, communication, and ongoing commitment to nurturing and cherishing the relationship God has blessed you with.

TAKE ACTION

1. **Schedule regular quality time together:**
   - Set aside dedicated time in your schedules for one-on-one time with your spouse. This could include date nights, shared hobbies, or even just uninterrupted conversations. Make it a non-negotiable commitment to prioritize this time and guard it against other distractions.
2. **Practice active listening and intentional communication:**
   - Show genuine interest in your spouse's thoughts, feelings, and experiences.
   - Practice active listening by giving your full attention, maintaining eye contact, and responding empathetically.
   - Create a safe space where your spouse feels heard, understood, and valued.
3. **Serve and support one another:**
   - Look for practical ways to serve and support your spouse.
   - Seek opportunities to alleviate their burdens, offer encouragement, and actively participate in their lives.
   - Demonstrate love and care through acts of kindness, selflessness, and sacrificial service, following the example of Christ's love for the church.

By scheduling regular quality time, practicing active listening, and actively serving and supporting one another, you can biblically encourage and prioritize each other in your marriage. These actions foster a deeper connection, strengthen the bond of love, and demonstrate the selflessness and love that Christ calls us to exhibit in our relationships.

PRAYER FOR HELP

Gracious Father, we humbly come before You, acknowledging the importance of prioritizing our spouse in our marriage. We ask for Your divine guidance and strength to help us make intentional choices and decisions that demonstrate our love and commitment to one another. Grant us the wisdom to invest our time, energy, and resources in ways that honor and prioritize our spouse, fostering a deeper bond and reflecting Your love in our relationship. Amen.

8

Remain Flexible And Adaptable

CHANGE

"Trust in the LORD with all your heart, and do not lean on your own understanding. In all your ways acknowledge him, and he will make straight your paths." Proverbs 3:5-6

REMAIN FLEXIBLE AND ADAPTABLE

In the past three-plus decades, we have lived in over a dozen homes in some six states. We have served in five-plus churches, taught classes, led conferences, and hosted both big and small groups in our home. We have experienced a number of job and career changes and have navigated educational pursuits to support it all. Add to that the arrival and raising of three children, each with their own unique personalities and needs. As parents, we pivoted ourselves for sports, dance, pageants, hobbies, schooling, relationships, jobs, and the launching of them into family life as young married adults with children. We have come to understand the value of not living too rigid a life.

Remaining flexible in a marriage relationship is essential because if one thing is constant in marriage, it is change. Along with all the changes in our family, we have experienced changes within ourselves as well. As you age, your likes, dislikes, preferences, and habits will change. You will experience new health and physical changes. Your family and friendships will take different shapes and sizes as relationships evolve over time. There will be things you expect to happen that don't, and things you did not expect to happen that will.

For Lisa and myself, we have always tried to find the balance between being rigid enough to have structure that includes planning, preparing, and executing. At the same time, we have never held our short-term, long-term, or lifetime plans too tightly. As Christians, perhaps the most valuable thing we have done is remaining open to the plans God has for us. Being open to God's plans enables us to be flexible and adapt to the changing circumstances of our lives. Proverbs 19:21 reminds us, 'Many are the plans in a person's heart, but it is the Lord's purpose that prevails.' Therefore, remaining open to God's leading ensures that our intentions and actions are always in alignment with His will.

QUICK REMINDER

By embracing changes in marriage, we align ourselves with God's purpose and plan for our lives. It requires a spirit of flexibility, openness, and a willingness to adapt to new circumstances. Embracing changes allows for the continued growth and deepening of love, unity, and shared experiences in our marriage. Through it all, we rely on God's guidance and trust in His faithfulness to lead us through every season of change.

GO DEEPER

Remaining flexible and adaptable in marriage is vital, as the Bible teaches us the importance of humility, selflessness, and unity within the marital relationship:

Ephesians 4:2-3: The apostle Paul encourages believers to "be completely humble and gentle; be patient, bearing with one another in love. Make every effort to keep the unity of the Spirit through the bond of peace." Flexibility and adaptability require humility, patience, and a willingness to adjust our expectations and preferences for the sake of unity and peace in the marriage.

Philippians 2:3-4: Paul instructs us to "do nothing out of selfish ambition or vain conceit. Rather, in humility value others above yourselves, not looking to your own interests but each of you to the interests of the others." Marriage calls us to prioritize our spouse's needs and interests, being willing to adapt our plans and desires to accommodate and serve one another.

Ecclesiastes 3:1: "For everything there is a season, and a time for every matter under heaven." Change is a natural part of life, including within the context of marriage. Embracing changes means recognizing that different seasons bring new challenges, opportunities, and growth for both individuals and the relationship.

By remaining flexible and adaptable, we embody biblical principles of humility, selflessness, and unity. It enables us to navigate the inevitable changes and challenges that come with marriage, fostering an environment of love, understanding, and growth. Ultimately, a flexible and adaptable mindset reflects our willingness to align our lives and choices with God's will, trusting Him to lead and guide us in our marital journey.

QUESTIONS FOR REFLECTION

1. **How am I currently responding to the changes happening in our marriage?**
   - Reflect on your own attitudes, emotions, and behaviors when faced with changes within your marriage. Are you resistant or open to embracing change?
   - Consider whether your response aligns with God's teachings and His desire for growth and transformation in your relationship.
2. **How can I support and encourage my spouse during times of change?**
   - Consider how you can be a source of strength, encouragement, and support to your spouse as they navigate changes in their life or within the marriage.

- Reflect on ways you can communicate love, understanding, and empathy during periods of transition or adjustment.

3. **What opportunities for growth and learning can we find in the midst of change?**
    - Embracing change often presents opportunities for personal and relational growth.
    - Reflect on how you and your spouse can learn and grow together through the changes you encounter.
    - Consider how you can view change as an opportunity to deepen your understanding of one another, strengthen your bond, and align your lives more closely with God's purposes.

By reflecting on these questions, you can gain insights into your own mindset and response to change, as well as identify areas where you can support and encourage your spouse. Embracing change in marriage requires a willingness to adapt, grow, and trust in God's guidance as you navigate the ever-changing seasons of life together.

TAKE ACTION

1. **Cultivate a mindset of openness and flexibility:**
    - Recognize that change is inevitable and approach it with a positive and open mindset.
    - Embrace the idea that change can bring new opportunities for growth, deeper connection, and shared experiences in your marriage.
    - Choose to view change as a chance to learn and adapt rather than a source of fear or resistance.
2. **Communicate openly and honestly:**

- ○ Foster an environment of open communication with your spouse, where you can share your thoughts, concerns, and emotions about the changes you are experiencing.
- ○ Listen actively and empathetically to your spouse's perspective. Seek to understand their feelings and needs, and express your own in a respectful and loving manner.

3. **Seek God's guidance and trust in His plan:**
   - ○ Turn to God in prayer and seek His guidance during times of change. Trust that He is with you and your spouse in every season and that He has a purpose and plan for your marriage.
   - ○ Lean on His wisdom and strength as you navigate the uncertainties and challenges that come with change, knowing that He is faithful to lead you through.

By cultivating a mindset of openness, communicating openly and honestly, and seeking God's guidance, you can actively embrace change and remain adaptable in your marriage. These actions foster resilience, unity, and trust as you navigate the ever-changing seasons of life together, allowing your marriage to thrive and grow according to God's perfect design.

PRAYER FOR HELP

Gracious Lord, we acknowledge the importance of remaining flexible and open to change in our marriages. We ask for Your divine guidance and strength to help us embrace the changes that come our way, trusting in Your plan for our relationship. Grant us the humility and willingness to adapt, the wisdom to navigate uncertainties, and the grace to support and uplift one another as we journey through life together. Amen.

9

Marriage Is A Lifelong Growth Process

GROWTH

"And we all, with unveiled face, beholding the glory of the Lord, are being transformed into the same image from one degree of glory to another. For this comes from the Lord who is the Spirit." 2 Corinthians 3:18

We understand marriage as a journey of continual learning and growth.

MARRIAGE IS A LIFELONG GROWTH PROCESS

Sanctification is indeed a 'churchy' term, but the principle is rather straightforward: when you become a Christian, your life is set on a course of growth to become more like Christ over a lifetime. Along this journey, there are what I would call 'mountaintops' and 'valleys' of growth. We often assume that our most significant growth occurs during the mountaintop moments—big, exciting, fun, and fulfilling times. However, what we have observed over the years, both individually and in our marriage, is that our most profound growth happens during the 'valley' moments of our lives.

Certainly, growth can occur during good times, successes, celebrations, and vacations. Nevertheless, our most significant growth emerges through challenging times such as failed attempts, hardships, losses, funerals, car accidents, and hospital visits. We've come to realize that our trials and difficulties serve as opportunities for spiritual and relational growth in our lives, ultimately shaping our marriage to align more closely with Christ's example.

"It's not that we long for difficulty, but our perspective on it has evolved over the years, much like our understanding of sanctification. When challenging times come, we now view them as opportunities for God to transform us, similar to the process of being molded and shaped into the image of our Savior, Christ Jesus, as described in 2 Corinthians 3:18. We see these trials as steps on the path to becoming more like Him.

QUICK REMINDER

We must be willing to learn from our experiences, seek wisdom from trusted sources, and invest in your personal development as individuals and as a couple. Sanctification in the context of a marriage relationship involves the ongoing process of becoming more Christ-like individually and as a couple. It is a journey of growth, transformation, and conformity to God's will for the union.

GO DEEPER

Sanctification in marriage entails pursuing holiness, love, and selflessness, as well as allowing the Holy Spirit to work in and through the relationship. Sanctification in marriage leads to a deepening intimacy, a greater reflection of Christ's love, and a mutual support in the journey of becoming more like Him together.

By prioritizing sanctification and growth together, couples create an environment that fosters spiritual intimacy, strengthens their relationship, and glorifies God. They support each other in their pursuit of holiness, providing accountability, encouragement, and grace.

Biblically, the importance of sanctification and growth together in marriage can be understood through several principles:

Unity and Oneness: In marriage, husband and wife are joined together as one in the sight of God (Genesis 2:24). As they grow individually in their sanctification, they also grow together in their spiritual journey. This shared pursuit of holiness strengthens their bond, deepens their understanding of each other, and aligns their lives with God's purposes for their marriage.

Mutual Edification: The Bible encourages believers to encourage and build one another up (1 Thessalonians 5:11). In a marital relationship, spouses have a unique opportunity to support and challenge each other in their spiritual growth. As they prioritize sanctification, they become instruments of God's grace in each other's lives, spurring one another on to love, good deeds, and spiritual maturity (Hebrews 10:24).

Reflecting Christ's Love: Marriage is a picture of the relationship between Christ and the Church (Ephesians 5:31-32). As spouses grow in sanctification, their love for one another becomes a reflection of Christ's sacrificial love. Through their pursuit of holiness, they bear witness to the transforming power of God's grace and become a testimony to the world of God's redemptive work in their lives.

As couples grow in Christ-likeness, they experience deeper joy, peace, and fulfillment in their marriage, becoming a source of blessing not only to each other but also to those around them.

QUESTIONS FOR REFLECTION

1. **How am I actively seeking to imitate Christ's character in my interactions with my spouse**
   - Reflect on the qualities of Christ's character, such as love, patience, forgiveness, and humility.
   - Ask yourself how you are intentionally embodying these attributes in your relationship with your spouse.
   - Consider specific situations or challenges where you can demonstrate Christlikeness and seek opportunities to grow in those areas.

2. **In what ways can I support and encourage my spouse's spiritual growth?**
   - Reflect on how you can be a source of support and encouragement for your spouse's journey of faith. Consider their spiritual needs, aspirations, and challenges.
   - Ask yourself how you can pray for and uplift them, provide accountability, and engage in activities that foster spiritual growth, such as studying the Bible together, attending worship services, or participating in a small group.

3. **Am I willing to submit my desires, preferences, and ambitions to God's will for my marriage?**
   - Reflect on your willingness to surrender your own desires and preferences to align with God's will for your marriage.
   - Ask yourself if you are seeking God's guidance in decision-making, prioritizing unity and selflessness over personal agendas.
   - Consider areas where you may be holding onto control or struggling to yield to God's plan, and invite Him to transform your heart and help you grow in submission and surrender.

These questions can serve as a starting point for self-reflection and growth in Christlikeness within your marriage. As you engage in honest introspection and seek God's guidance, you can cultivate a deeper understanding of how to walk in the footsteps of Christ and foster spiritual growth within your relationship.

TAKE ACTION

1. **Prioritize Daily Spiritual Practices:**
   - Make intentional efforts to prioritize daily spiritual practices that deepen your relationship with God. This can

include regular prayer, studying the Bible individually and together as a couple, engaging in meaningful worship, and practicing gratitude. By nurturing your own spiritual growth, you'll be better equipped to reflect Christ's character in your marriage.

2. **Cultivate a Spirit of Humility and Forgiveness:**
    - Embrace humility and forgiveness as foundational principles in your marriage.
    - Practice humility by considering your spouse's needs, perspectives, and feelings above your own.
    - Be quick to extend forgiveness, just as Christ has forgiven you.
    - Seek reconciliation and restoration whenever conflicts arise, and let love guide your actions and responses.

3. **Serve and Love Unconditionally:**
    - Follow Christ's example of selfless love and service. Look for opportunities to serve your spouse, not only in grand gestures but also in the small acts of kindness and thoughtfulness.
    - Seek to understand and meet their needs, even when it requires sacrifice.
    - Choose to love unconditionally, extending grace and compassion in moments of weakness or mistakes.

By implementing these action steps, you will create an environment that fosters growth in Christlikeness within your marriage. Remember, growth takes time and patience, so be gentle with yourself and your spouse as you navigate this journey together. Trust in God's transformative work and rely on His strength to help you grow in reflecting the love, humility, forgiveness, and selflessness of Christ in your marriage.

PRAYER FOR HELP

Heavenly Father, we lift our hearts to You, seeking Your divine guidance and presence as we desire to grow spiritually in our marriage. Grant us the wisdom and discernment to prioritize our relationship with You, allowing Your Word to shape our thoughts, words, and actions. Strengthen the bond between us as we seek to honor You and grow in faith together, drawing closer to You and to one another each day. Amen.

10

Serve Each Other

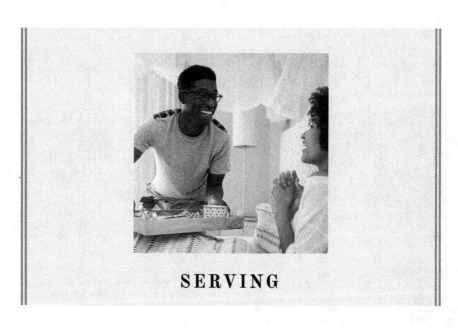

SERVING

"Each of you should use whatever gift you have received to serve others, as faithful stewards of God's grace in its various forms. If anyone speaks, they should do so as one who speaks the very words of God. If anyone serves, they should do so with the strength God provides, so that in all things God may be praised through Jesus Christ." 1 Peter 4:10-11

SERVE EACH OTHER

I can tell my wife how beautiful she is, and she truly is. I can express my gratitude for a wonderful meal or her effort in making my favorite treat, and I always am grateful. I can plan date nights or organize our next vacation getaway, and I do. I can even surprise her with a bouquet of beautiful flowers, which I occasionally do. But the truth is, all of this might be in vain if I forget to take the trash cans to the curb before Friday morning or leave the bed unmade when I'm the last one out. My wife interprets care and concern mainly through the acts of service lens. This is partly because it is her love language; she serves others. She's constantly considering me, our children, our grandchildren, her family, her friends, and even strangers to see if she might be able to serve them in some way.

In marriage, we swiftly transition from the pronoun "me" to "we" and from "mine" to "ours." Serving in marriage is marked by closely watching your spouse, recognizing their needs, and taking action to meet those needs, often in a sacrificial or unexpected way. Many times, it involves setting aside your own personal needs and desires to be available and assist your spouse with their needs. Serving one another is an act of humility that says, "I'm willing to put you first and consider how I can prioritize your needs over my own."

Ultimately, in marriage, when we serve each other, we get a chance to strengthen the bonds of love and build a deep connection that goes beyond words and gestures. It's a way of saying, "I value you, I cherish our relationship, and I am committed to making your life better." When we serve each other, we create a partnership based on mutual care and selflessness, fostering a sense of security and trust within the marriage.

It's essential to recognize that serving each other in marriage is not about keeping score or expecting something in return. Truly serving each other is a genuine and selfless expression of love. When we both adopt this attitude of service, a beautiful cycle of care and support is established. This makes our marriage a place of refuge and happiness where we can both thrive and grow together. In serving each other, we find joy in knowing that we are actively contributing to the well-being and happiness of our spouse, which, in turn, enriches our own lives.

QUICK REMINDER

The Bible encourages believers to utilize the gifts and talents we have received from God to serve others. In the context of marriage, it reminds spouses to employ their unique abilities to bless and support one another, fostering a spirit of selflessness and care.

GO DEEPER

The value of serving one another in marriage is deeply rooted in the teachings of Jesus Christ. Throughout the Bible, we see the importance of selflessness, humility, and putting others' needs before our own. When spouses serve each other in love, they demonstrate Christ's love to one another and create an environment of mutual support, care, and growth.

Jesus Himself exemplified the value of serving others. In Mark 10:45 (NIV), He said, "For even the Son of Man did not come to be served, but to serve, and to give his life as a ransom for many." Jesus's sacrificial service on the cross shows the depth of His love for humanity. As followers of Christ, we are called to imitate His example and serve one another with the same selflessness and love.

Serving is an act of humility. In Galatians 5:13 (NIV), the Apostle Paul writes, "You, my brothers and sisters, were called to be free. But do not use your freedom to indulge the flesh; rather, serve one another humbly in love." This verse highlights the freedom we have in Christ and emphasizes that this freedom should be expressed through loving service to others, including our spouses.

Serving one another in marriage brings numerous benefits. It fosters an atmosphere of mutual respect, understanding, and appreciation. It strengthens the bond between spouses, builds trust, and promotes unity. When couples serve one another, they demonstrate Christ's love to the world, serving as a witness to the transforming power of God's grace in their lives.

By serving each other in marriage, spouses actively seek opportunities to meet each other's needs, both practical and emotional. They support each other's dreams, aspirations, and spiritual growth. Serving one another also involves forgiveness, patience, and bearing with one another's weaknesses, creating an environment of grace and acceptance.

Ultimately, the value of serving one another in marriage is rooted in the commandment to love one another as Christ has loved us (John 13:34). By embodying Christ's selfless love and serving one another, couples can experience a deeper connection, a stronger marriage, and a reflection of God's love in their relationship.

QUESTIONS FOR REFLECTION

1. **How well am I truly aware of my spouse's needs, desires, and challenges?**
   - How can I actively seek to understand them better in order to serve them more effectively?
2. **What are some specific ways I can consistently demonstrate love and service to my spouse**
   - How can I make intentional efforts to prioritize their well-being and happiness in our daily interactions?
3. **In what areas of our marriage do I tend to struggle in serving my spouse?**
   - How can I overcome any obstacles, such as selfishness or neglect, in order to better serve and support them?

TAKE ACTION

1. **Practice active listening and empathy:**
   - Make a conscious effort to truly listen and understand your spouse's thoughts, feelings, and needs.
   - Show empathy by putting yourself in their shoes and seeking to understand their perspective. This will help you respond with compassion and serve them in a way that addresses their specific needs.
2. **Prioritize intentional acts of kindness:**
   - Look for opportunities to perform small acts of kindness and service for your spouse on a regular basis.
   - It could be as simple as preparing their favorite meal, offering a word of encouragement, or taking care of a task they usually handle. These gestures of love and service

help foster a culture of mutual care and support in your marriage.

3. **Communicate openly and collaborate:**

   ○ Regularly discuss with your spouse how you can better serve and support each other.

   ○ Share your desires, concerns, and needs, and encourage your spouse to do the same.

   ○ Collaborate on finding practical solutions and strategies that enable both of you to serve each other more effectively.

   ○ By working together, you can create a strong foundation of mutual service and grow in your ability to meet each other's needs.

PRAYER FOR HELP

Heavenly Father, we come before you humbly, acknowledging our need for your guidance and strength in serving one another in our marriage. Grant us the wisdom to understand each other's needs and the selflessness to meet them wholeheartedly. Fill our hearts with your love, so that we may serve each other with joy, grace, and compassion, reflecting your love in our actions. Amen.

11

Honesty Is A Non-Negotiable

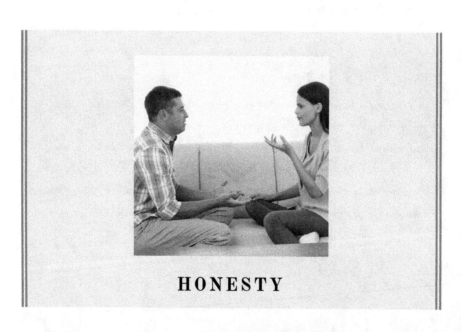

HONESTY

"Therefore each of you must put off falsehood and speak truthfully to your neighbor, for we are all members of one body." Ephesians 4:25

HONESTY IS A NON-NEGOTIABLE

Several years ago, I developed four triage questions that I ask every couple with whom I begin a marriage counseling relationship. One of those questions is, 'Do you trust your spouse to be honest with you about all things, big and small?' I see this as a critical question because I don't believe you can have a marriage without trust. I consider honesty and trust to be non-negotiable pillars that must be present in a marriage. You can't love someone you don't trust. Without trust, a marriage lacks a solid foundation, making it vulnerable to instability, doubt, and insecurity.

Honesty is a marriage's vulnerability. You have to be willing to tell the truth even when, for various reasons, you may find it difficult to do so. For honesty in marriage to survive, it must often be met with grace, understanding, and even empathy. If your spouse commits to honesty and truth-telling, and it is met with harsh and critical judgment, honesty tends to withdraw and disappear. Honesty must be met with grace, understanding, and empathy, as harsh judgment will simply undermine the integrity of honesty in a marriage. In a healthy marriage, the equation is simple: if you truly love me, you will tell me the truth, and I can trust you.

QUICK REMINDER

Trust is the most important ingredient in any relationship, but it can be very fragile. It takes time to build yet can be destroyed in an instant. It is, however, the glue of any meaningful connection with another person.

Whether we identify it in this way or not, trust is clearly the most important factor in helping couples and individuals build strong, lasting, loving relationships. With it, couples feel safe with each other, and they communicate what's in their heart, resolve problems, and enjoy every aspect of their relationship, including their sex life in marriage. But without it, every interaction becomes a manipulative dance to control the other person's behavior.

GO DEEPER

Biblically, honesty is essential in a trusting marriage relationship because it aligns with God's nature and character. The Bible teaches that God is a God of truth, and His desire is for His people to walk in truth and honesty. Honesty fosters trust, openness, and vulnerability, which are vital components of a strong and healthy marriage.

Honesty builds Trust: Proverbs 12:22 (NIV) states, "The Lord detests lying lips, but he delights in people who are trustworthy." This verse emphasizes that honesty is pleasing to God, while deceit and falsehood are detestable to Him. Honesty builds a foundation of integrity and righteousness, promoting a loving and secure environment within the marriage.

Speaking truthfully to our greatest neighbor: Ephesians 4:25 (NIV) exhorts believers, "Therefore each of you must put off falsehood and speak truthfully to your neighbor, for we are all members of one body." In the context of marriage, spouses are not only neighbors but also intimately connected as "one flesh" (Genesis 2:24). Honesty and truthfulness in communication are essential for understanding, resolving conflicts, and building a strong marital bond.

God desires truthfulness: In addition, Psalm 51:6 (NIV) says, "Surely you desire truth in the inner parts; you teach me wisdom in the inmost place." This verse reminds us that God desires truthfulness not only in our outward actions but also in the depths of our hearts. Honesty cultivates intimacy and emotional safety in marriage, allowing spouses to truly know and understand one another.

By being honest with our spouse, we honor God's commandments, build trust, and foster emotional intimacy. Honesty enables us to freely share our thoughts, feelings, and struggles, creating an environment where conflicts can be resolved with understanding and grace. It also provides an opportunity for growth, accountability, and mutual support in our journey of becoming more like Christ. Ultimately, honesty in marriage reflects the truth and authenticity that God desires for our relationships.

QUESTIONS FOR REFLECTION

1. **Am I consistently practicing honesty and truthfulness in my communication with my spouse?**
   - Are there any areas where I tend to withhold information or distort the truth?
2. **How does my level of honesty impact the trust and emotional intimacy in our marriage?**
   - Are there any past instances where my lack of honesty has caused damage or strained the relationship?
3. **Am I creating a safe and non-judgmental space for my spouse to be honest with me?**
   - How can I encourage open and transparent communication, where both of us feel comfortable sharing our thoughts, feelings, and struggles without fear of judgment or rejection?

TAKE ACTION

1. **Cultivate a culture of open communication:**
   - Create an atmosphere in your marriage where honesty is valued and encouraged.
   - Make a commitment to listen actively and non-judgmentally to your spouse, allowing them to express themselves honestly.
   - Foster an environment where both partners feel safe and comfortable sharing their thoughts, feelings, and concerns.

2. **Practice vulnerability and transparency:**
   - Be willing to be vulnerable and transparent with your spouse.
   - Share your thoughts, feelings, and experiences openly, even when it may be challenging or uncomfortable. This sets an example for your spouse to do the same and promotes an honest and authentic connection between you both.

3. **Address and resolve conflicts with honesty:**
   - When conflicts arise, approach them with a commitment to honesty.
   - Avoid defensiveness, and instead, strive to understand your spouse's perspective and express your own feelings and needs truthfully.
   - Work together to find mutually beneficial solutions, seeking resolution with honesty, humility, and a desire to grow both individually and as a couple.

By practicing these action steps, you can create a foundation of honesty in your marriage, fostering trust, emotional intimacy, and a strong partnership built on transparency and authenticity.

PRAYER FOR HELP

Dear Heavenly Father, we come before you seeking your guidance and strength to practice honesty and build trust in our marriage. Help us to be open and transparent with one another, sharing our thoughts, feelings, and struggles without fear of judgment or rejection. Grant us the wisdom and courage to cultivate a relationship rooted in truth, where trust can flourish, and our love for one another can deepen. Amen.

12

Commitment Is Marriage Glue

COMMITMENT

"To the married I give this charge (not I, but the Lord): the wife should not separate from her husband (but if she does, she should remain unmarried or else be reconciled to her husband), and the husband should not divorce his wife." 1 Corinthians 7:10–11

COMMITMENT IS MARRIAGE GLUE

Sometimes, I believe the reason Lisa and I have made it this far is that we are simply too stubborn to give up on each other. We have never fully figured it all out, but one thing we have figured out is that we are not going anywhere. I told Lisa long ago, 'If you leave me, I'm going with you!'

Commitment in our age has fallen on hard times, and we tend to live in a disposable society. We say we will, and we often don't, and when things are broken, we often find it easier to just throw them away. Unfortunately, this disposable, low commitment mentality has led many couples to live with the constant threat of the abandonment of the relationship, and divorce is always on the table. We have couples who submit marriage counseling requests, and in the request, it will say something like this: 'We would like to come in for counseling and see if we should stay together or get a divorce.' Listen, in a broken and sinful world, divorce is always a possibility for any marriage, but for a committed marriage, the first decision we make is that divorce is not an option.

I know there are non-negotiables, as well as Biblical grounds for divorce. We don't just learn to live with unrepentant adultery or other sinfully abusive actions from our spouse. I also know that no sin demands divorce, since God can bring confession, repentance, and healing in any situation. The truth is, however, I find as a marriage counselor that most offenses fall far short of serious offenses but are rather tied to a simple lack of commitment. Let return to our word being our work and commit to fixing what is broken, and thereby remain steadfast to working hard on healing and restoring our some-times broken marriages.

QUICK REMINDER

The Bible encourages couples to remain committed to their marriage vows and to prioritize their covenant relationship, it does not promote or endorse the idea of threatening to abandon the marriage. Instead, the biblical perspective emphasizes the importance of love, forgiveness, and reconciliation in marital relationships.

GO DEEPER

Ephesians 4:32 urges believers to "be kind to one another, tender-hearted, forgiving one another, as God in Christ forgave you." This verse highlights the call to extend grace and forgiveness to our spouses, seeking reconciliation and healing rather than resorting to threats or abandonment.

In 1 Corinthians 13:4-7, often referred to as the "love chapter," the apostle Paul describes the qualities of love, including patience, kindness, and perseverance. These virtues are meant to guide our actions and attitudes within marriage, fostering an environment of love, understanding, and commitment.

Additionally, Jesus teaches about the sanctity of marriage in Matthew 19:6, stating, "What therefore God has joined together, let not man separate." This verse emphasizes the permanence of the marital bond and discourages actions or attitudes that would seek to break that bond.

Rather than resorting to threats or abandonment, biblical principles encourage couples to seek reconciliation, open communication, and to work through challenges together. Marriage is a sacred commitment, and it is in the context of this commitment that couples can experience growth, healing, and the fulfillment of God's purposes for their union.

Biblically, the value of being committed to the marriage covenant is rooted in God's design and purpose for marriage. In Genesis 2:24, God established the foundation of marriage, declaring, "Therefore a man shall leave his father and his mother and hold fast to his wife, and they shall become one flesh." This verse emphasizes the unity and permanence of the marital bond.

Jesus reaffirmed the sanctity of marriage and the importance of commitment in Matthew 19:6, saying, "So they are no longer two but one flesh. What therefore God has joined together, let not man separate." This verse highlights that marriage is a sacred union orchestrated by God Himself, and it is not to be taken lightly or easily dissolved.

The Apostle Paul further emphasizes the value of commitment in marriage in Ephesians 5:25, where he instructs husbands to love their wives as Christ loved the church, giving Himself up for her. This sacrificial love requires unwavering commitment, just as Christ's love for the church is steadfast and unchanging.

Being committed to the marriage covenant demonstrates obedience to God's commands and reflects His unchanging faithfulness. It provides a solid foundation for the relationship, fostering trust, security, and intimacy. Through commitment, spouses can weather the storms of life together, grow in love, and fulfill the purpose of marriage to glorify God and build a lifelong partnership.

QUESTIONS FOR REFLECTION

1. **Am I truly prioritizing and honoring the commitment I made to my spouse and to God when we entered into the marriage covenant?**
   - How can I actively demonstrate my commitment in both words and actions?
2. **In what areas of my marriage do I find it most challenging to remain committed?**
   - Are there specific situations, conflicts, or struggles that test my commitment?
   - How can I seek God's guidance and strength to navigate and overcome these challenges?
3. **How does my commitment to my marriage covenant align with my understanding of God's design and purpose for marriage?**
   - How can I deepen my understanding of the biblical principles and values that underpin the importance of commitment, and how can I apply them more intentionally in my relationship?

These reflective questions can help individuals assess their level of commitment to their marriage covenant, identify areas for growth and improvement, and seek God's guidance in remaining steadfast in their commitment to their spouse.

TAKE ACTION

1. **Make a conscious decision to prioritize your marriage:**

○ Commitment starts with a deliberate choice to prioritize your spouse and your marriage above other competing priorities.

○ Set aside time, energy, and effort to invest in your relationship, even when life gets busy or challenging.

1. **Foster a culture of mutual respect and understanding:**

   ○ Treat your spouse with kindness, respect, and empathy.

   ○ Seek to understand their perspective, listen attentively, and validate their feelings and experiences.

   ○ Practice forgiveness and grace, recognizing that no one is perfect.

   ○ Cultivate an environment of love, acceptance, and support.

2. **Continuously invest in your relationship:**

   ○ Commitment requires ongoing effort and investment.

   ○ Engage in activities that strengthen your bond, such as regular date nights, shared hobbies, or pursuing common goals.

   ○ Regularly communicate and connect with each other, expressing appreciation, affection, and affirmation.

   ○ Seek opportunities for personal and spiritual growth, both individually and as a couple.

By taking these action steps, you actively cultivate commitment in your marriage. It involves intentional choices, fostering a positive and respectful atmosphere, and consistently investing in the growth and well-being of your relationship.

PRAYER FOR HELP

Dear Heavenly Father, we come before you with grateful hearts for the gift of marriage. We humbly ask for your help in staying committed to our marriage vows and honoring the covenant we made before you. Grant us the strength, wisdom, and grace to navigate challenges, grow together, and remain steadfast in our love and commitment for one another. Amen.

13

Work On Fixing Yourself - Not Your Spouse

CHANGE

"Why do you look at the speck of sawdust in your brother's eye and pay no attention to the plank in your own eye? How can you say to your brother, 'Let me take the speck out of your eye,' when all the time there is a plank in your own eye? You hypocrite, first take the plank out of your own

eye, and then you will see clearly to remove the speck from your brother's eye." Matthew 7:3-5

WORK ON FIXING YOURSELF - NOT YOUR SPOUSE

As a marriage counselor, one of the four questions I ask during my intake triage is, "What must change in actions and attitudes for this marriage to survive and thrive moving forward?" I carefully observe the number of "he/she" responses versus "I/we" responses I receive from each spouse. The truth is, I have learned to pay close attention to how much the spouse believes that fixing their partner is the key to marital happiness.

The difference sounds something like this: "She is going to have to stop spending so much time on her phone and start spending time with me doing things that I like to do" versus "I wish that together we would spend less time on our devices and television and invest time exploring activities we both enjoy doing."

Here's the thing—I am always quite sure that both spouses, with God's help, will need to make some changes to improve the marriage. I am equally convinced that they can't change each other. If a couple views the problems in the marriage as "our" problems, then they are already on the teamwork side of marriage. However, when one is dug in against the other and stuck in the finger-pointing mode, it becomes clear that it is a declaration of war and not a peace treaty they have come to counseling for.

QUICK REMINDER

Biblically, the responsibility to focus on personal accountability in the marriage relationship is rooted in the teachings of Jesus and the principle of self-examination. In Matthew 7:3-5, Jesus urges individuals to first examine themselves before seeking to address the faults of others. This principle applies to marriage, emphasizing the importance of personal growth and self-reflection.

GO DEEPER

The Apostle Paul also emphasizes personal accountability in Philippians 2:12, urging believers to "work out [their] own salvation with fear and trembling." This verse highlights the individual responsibility to pursue spiritual growth and maturity.

Focusing on personal accountability in the marriage relationship allows each spouse to take ownership of their actions, attitudes, and areas for improvement. It fosters humility, self-awareness, and personal growth, which can positively impact the dynamics of the relationship.

Rather than focusing on changing each other, biblical wisdom encourages individuals to focus on their own transformation through the power of the Holy Spirit. This does not mean ignoring or enabling harmful behavior but recognizing that lasting change comes from within and is facilitated by personal responsibility, prayer, and reliance on God's transformative work in our lives.

By prioritizing personal accountability, individuals can cultivate a healthier and more fulfilling marriage, as they become more aligned with God's principles and grow in Christlikeness.

One passage that encourages us to seek God to change and transform our hearts is Psalm 51:10: "Create in me a clean heart, O God, and renew a right spirit within me." This verse reflects King David's plea to God for inner transformation and a renewed heart after his repentance for his sins. It acknowledges our need for God's intervention to purify and change us from within.

Another passage is Ezekiel 36:26: "And I will give you a new heart, and a new spirit I will put within you. And I will remove the heart of stone from your flesh and give you a heart of flesh." In this verse, God promises to give His people a new heart, symbolizing a transformation of their inner being through His grace and power.

Additionally, 2 Corinthians 5:17 states, "Therefore, if anyone is in Christ, he is a new creation. The old has passed away; behold, the new has come." This verse highlights the transformative power of being in Christ. Through our faith in Him, we can experience a radical change and become a new creation, with our hearts and lives transformed by His love and grace.

These passages remind us of our dependence on God to change and transform our hearts. They inspire us to humbly seek Him, surrendering our will and allowing Him to work in us, shaping us into the image of Christ. Through prayer, repentance, and a sincere desire for God's transformative power, we invite His loving presence to bring about lasting change in our hearts and lives.

QUESTIONS FOR REFLECTION

1. **Am I spending more time and energy trying to change my spouse rather than focusing on my own personal growth and transformation?**
   - How can I redirect my efforts towards seeking God's work in my own heart and life?
2. **Do I trust in God's ability to change hearts and work in my spouse's life, or do I take on the role of a fixer, trying to control or manipulate their behaviors and attitudes?**

○ How can I surrender control and rely on God's timing and process in their life?

3. **Am I seeking God's guidance and wisdom in areas where I desire change in my spouse?**

○ How can I pray for their transformation with humility and a genuine concern for their well-being, rather than attempting to mold them into my own image or preferences?

These reflective questions can help individuals assess their focus and intentions in their marriage. They encourage self-examination, surrendering control to God, and seeking His guidance in their own personal growth rather than solely trying to change their spouse.

TAKE ACTION

1. **Seek God's guidance and transformation through prayer:**
   ○ Regularly spend time in prayer, seeking God's wisdom and guidance in areas where you desire change.
   ○ Humbly ask Him to reveal any areas of your heart that need transformation and invite the Holy Spirit to work in you.
   ○ Ask for the strength and grace to align your heart and desires with God's will.

2. **Engage in self-reflection and introspection:**
   ○ Set aside time for self-reflection to honestly assess your thoughts, attitudes, and behaviors. Identify areas where you may need to let go of pride, selfishness, or unhealthy patterns.
   ○ Seek opportunities for personal growth, such as reading scripture, engaging in spiritual disciplines, or seeking counsel from a trusted mentor or counselor.

3. **Take practical steps towards change:**
   - Once you have identified areas for growth, develop an action plan to actively work on transforming your heart. This may involve setting specific goals, implementing healthy habits, and seeking accountability from a trusted friend or spouse.
   - Be open to feedback and constructive criticism, and make a commitment to follow through with your intentions.

By taking these action steps, you demonstrate a proactive commitment to personal growth and transformation. As you prioritize changing your own heart, you create an environment that encourages growth and inspires positive change in your marriage and relationships.

PRAYER FOR HELP

Dear Heavenly Father, I humbly come before you, acknowledging my need for personal transformation and growth. Grant me the wisdom and strength to take accountability for my own heart and actions. Help me surrender control to you and rely on your guidance, that I may align my heart with yours and experience the transformative power of your love. Amen.

14

There Is An Enemy - It's
Not Your Spouse

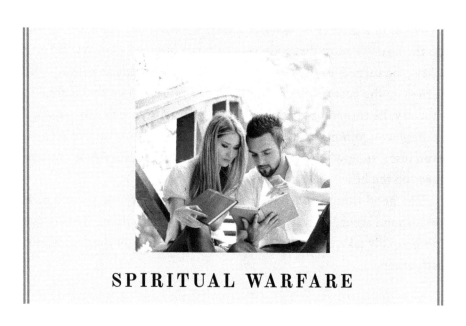

SPIRITUAL WARFARE

"For our struggle is not against flesh and blood, but against the rulers, against the authorities, against the powers of this dark world and against the spiritual forces of evil in the heavenly realms." Ephesians 6:12

THERE IS AN ENEMY - IT'S NOT YOUR SPOUSE

The enemy has come to steal, kill, and destroy, and that is exactly what he wants to do to our marriages. Interestingly, one of his greatest tactics is not to attack either of you but to get you to attack each other. Occasionally, in our marital conflicts, we step back and realize that the enemy is trying his best to convince each of us that the other is the enemy.

Another thing we have come to realize in many years of marriage is that when God is up to something in our lives, when He is ready to use us in a greater capacity, it always appears that the enemy turns up the heat. We can distinctly recall shortly after we gave our lives to Christ, he turned up the heat. After I accepted a calling as a deacon, he turned up the heat. After surrendering our careers to serve full-time in ministry, he turned up the heat. And it seems always prior to marriage conferences, joining or starting new small groups, ministry moves, or even just a time when we decide to start a new couples devotional, he turns up the heat.

The good thing is we have come to see it for what it is, and now we respond accordingly. Rather than going to war with each other, we more rapidly take up the whole armor of God and fight the enemy, not each other.

QUICK REMINDER

Biblically, the reality that our battles in marriage are more spiritual battles and not against our spouse is highlighted in Ephesians 6:12, which states, "For our struggle is not against flesh and blood, but against the rulers, against the authorities, against the powers of this dark world and against the spiritual forces of evil in the heavenly realms." This verse reminds us that the conflicts and challenges we face in our relationships are often rooted in spiritual warfare rather than solely personal or relational issues.

GO DEEPER

Understanding that our battles in marriage are primarily spiritual helps us approach them with a God-centered perspective, recognizing the need to rely on His strength, seek His guidance, and apply His principles in resolving conflicts and overcoming challenges. It shifts our focus from blaming or attacking our spouse to recognizing the spiritual dynamics at play and responding with love, grace, and spiritual discernment.

2 Corinthians 10:3-5 teaches us that our weapons in these spiritual battles are not of the world, but mighty through God to pull down strongholds and take every thought captive to the obedience of Christ. This indicates that our focus should be on spiritual strategies such as prayer, seeking God's guidance, and aligning our thoughts and actions with His Word.

God's intention for marriage is to create a partnership where two individuals come together as one. Genesis 2:24 states, "Therefore a man shall leave his father and his mother and hold fast to his wife, and they shall become one flesh." This unity in marriage signifies a shared purpose and a commitment to facing life's challenges together.

Additionally, Ecclesiastes 4:9-12 speaks of the strength and support that comes from companionship: "Two are better than one... For if they fall, one will lift up his fellow. But woe to him who is alone when he falls and has not another to lift him up!" This verse emphasizes the importance of having a partner who stands with us in the battles of life, providing encouragement, support, and strength.

Moreover, 1 Peter 3:7 encourages husbands and wives to live with understanding and honor, recognizing that they are heirs together of the grace of life. This verse reminds us that our spouse is not our adversary, but a fellow recipient of God's grace, with whom we can navigate life's challenges and grow in faith.

By understanding our spouse as our companion in the battle, we approach marriage with a mindset of unity, support, and mutual respect. We can face the spiritual battles together, relying on each other's strengths, and offering love and encouragement as we grow in our relationship with God and navigate life's challenges hand in hand.

QUESTIONS FOR REFLECTION

1. **Am I aware of the spiritual battles that exist in my marriage?**
   - How am I actively seeking to discern and address these spiritual battles instead of solely focusing on the surface-level conflicts?

2. **How am I nurturing my own spiritual life and relationship with God in order to effectively fight spiritual battles in my marriage?**
   - Am I spending time in prayer, studying God's Word, and seeking His guidance and wisdom in addressing challenges?

3. **How am I intentionally partnering with my spouse in prayer and spiritual warfare?**
   - How can we together seek God's protection, guidance, and victory in the spiritual battles we face as a couple?

TAKE ACTION

1. **Prioritize prayer together:**
   - Make prayer a regular and intentional practice in your marriage.
   - Set aside specific times to pray together, seeking God's guidance, protection, and strength in facing spiritual battles.
   - Pray for each other's spiritual growth, discernment, and victory over the enemy's schemes.

2. **Study and apply God's Word together:**
   - Engage in regular Bible study and discussion as a couple.
   - Explore scriptures that address spiritual warfare, marital unity, and God's promises.
   - Seek to understand and apply God's principles in your lives, using His Word as a weapon against the enemy's lies and temptations.

3. **Cultivate a supportive and accountable community:**
   - Surround yourselves with other believers who can provide support, encouragement, and accountability in your spiritual journey.
   - Join a couples' Bible study group, seek mentorship from a mature Christian couple, or become part of a church community that fosters spiritual growth.
   - Together, create a safe space to share struggles, seek advice, and pray for one another's spiritual well-being.

By taking these action steps, couples can actively fight spiritual battles together, strengthening their spiritual bond and relying on God's power to overcome challenges. They foster an environment of unity, prayer, and growth, ensuring that both partners are equipped and supported in their spiritual journey.

PRAYER FOR HELP

Dear Heavenly Father, we come before you humbly, recognizing our need for your guidance and strength in the spiritual battles we face as a couple. Grant us the wisdom to discern the enemy's tactics and the discernment to navigate through the challenges that arise. Fill us with your Holy Spirit, empowering us to stand firm in faith, to seek your will above all else, and to experience victory as we trust in your unfailing love. Amen.

15

Getting Help Is A Good Thing

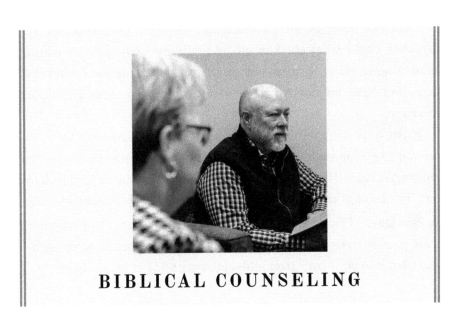

BIBLICAL COUNSELING

"I myself am convinced, my brothers and sisters, that you yourselves are full of goodness, filled with knowledge and competent to instruct one another." Romans 15:14

GETTING HELP IS A GOOD THING

Going to speak to a Marriage Counselor is not easy. Even being willing to take the step to getting help is vulnerable. And then, once you decide to do it, you are faced with endless options such as who, what kind, short-term, long-term, intensives, couples-based, male, female, team, secular, integrationist, or Biblical counselors. Then there are cost considerations, schedules, perhaps babysitters. Also, it is going to take effort, work, listening, doing, starting some things and stopping some as well.

I am not here to critique other counseling professionals or approaches. I have many good friends and colleagues who provide marital counseling in many formats with numerous techniques and interventions and have no doubt helped many couples navigate a healthier marriage.

However, I don't think it would surprise you if I advocated for Biblical Marriage Counseling. See, I believe since God created marriage, that His people using His Word have the blueprint for how it is to be lived out. The Biblical counselor is but an *Instrument in the Redeemer's Hand*, as Paul David Tripp eloquently wrote. But His hand is the best one to trust your marriage in. Don't delay—you have waited long enough—and tried it in your own strength—reach out and get help today!

QUICK REMINDER

Through the indwelling of the Holy Spirit, believers are filled with goodness, which refers to the fruit of the Spirit mentioned in Galatians 5:22-23. Qualities, such as love, patience, kindness, and gentleness, enable us to provide wise and compassionate counsel to others.

As followers of Christ, we have access to the knowledge of God's Word through Scripture and the teachings of the church. This knowledge equips us to provide biblical guidance and instruction to one another, helping each other grow in faith, navigate challenges, and find godly solutions.

GO DEEPER

Romans 15:14 further affirms that within the body of Christ, we are not alone in our journey of faith. We can draw upon the spiritual resources and experiences of fellow believers to offer encouragement, support, and counsel. It reminds us that our role as members of the church is not only to receive counseling but also to be active participants in counseling and instructing one another as we share our faith, wisdom, and understanding of God's Word.

Therefore, Romans 15:14 assures us that, as members of the church, we have the capacity and responsibility to provide counsel and support to one another, drawing on the goodness, knowledge, and wisdom that God has graciously given us through His Spirit and His Word.

Several other passages support the practice of counseling each other in and through the life of the church:

Proverbs 11:14 states, "Where there is no guidance, a people falls, but in an abundance of counselors, there is safety." God's church and biblical counselors can provide the necessary guidance, wisdom, and support during challenging seasons of marriage. They can offer biblical perspectives, prayerful guidance, and practical advice based on God's Word.

Ephesians 4:11-13: "And he gave the apostles, the prophets, the evangelists, the shepherds and teachers, to equip the saints for the work of ministry, for building up the body of Christ, until we all attain to the unity of the faith and of the knowledge of the Son of God." The church is equipped with gifted individuals who are called to shepherd and teach God's people. Seeking counseling through the church allows couples to access this God-given ministry for their growth, healing, and restoration.

The church is called to support and uplift one another in times of difficulty. Seeking counseling through the church provides an opportunity for couples to share their burdens and receive the compassionate care and guidance of their brothers and sisters in Christ.

While formal biblical counseling has its place, it is important to recognize that God can also use one-on-one member care within the church to provide support and encouragement. Here are a few ways we can understand this:

The "one another" commands in the New Testament: Throughout the New Testament, there are various instructions for believers to care for and support one another. For example, Romans 12:10 says, "Love one another with brotherly affection. Outdo one another in showing honor." These commands emphasize the importance of personal relationships and individual care within the body of believers.

The example of the early church: In the early church, we see a sense of community and mutual support among believers. Acts 2:42-47 describes how the believers devoted themselves to fellowship, prayer, and caring for one another's needs. This indicates that personal, one-on-one care and support were essential components of their spiritual journey.

Galatians 6:2: "Bear one another's burdens, and so fulfill the law of Christ." This verse highlights the responsibility we have as believers to walk alongside one another, offering care and support in times of difficulty. It suggests a more personal and individualized approach to supporting and encouraging fellow believers.

In addition to formal biblical counseling, one-on-one member care allows for a deeper level of connection and understanding within the church community. It involves coming alongside one another, listening, praying, and providing practical assistance when needed. It acknowledges that God can work through the caring relationships and genuine concern of fellow believers to bring comfort, healing, and support.

By recognizing the value of one-on-one member care, we can foster a culture of compassion and support within the church, where individuals feel loved, valued, and encouraged in their faith journey.

QUESTIONS FOR REFLECTION

1. **Am I willing to humble myself and seek help from others in the church for the challenges in my marriage?**
2. **Do I believe that God can work through the guidance and counsel of biblically trained individuals within the church to bring healing and restoration to my marriage?**
3. **Am I actively seeking out the resources and opportunities available in my church community to receive biblically-based counseling and care for my marriage?**
   - Am i engaged in a small group, attending marriage conferences, and engaging in the life of the church as a means of encouragement and support for my marriage.

These questions encourage self-reflection and assessment of one's openness to seeking help, trust in God's work through the church, and engagement in actively pursuing the support available within the church community. They help individuals evaluate their readiness and willingness to seek biblical counseling and care for their marriage, which is an important step towards seeking the help they may need.

TAKE ACTION

1. **Pray and seek God's guidance:**
   - Begin by praying and seeking God's wisdom and direction in your marriage struggles.
   - Ask Him to lead you to the right people and resources within your church community that can provide the support and guidance you need.
2. **Reach out to church leaders:**
   - Approach your pastor, elders, or trusted church leaders to share your concerns and seek their guidance. They can provide spiritual counsel, recommend resources, and connect you with individuals who are trained in biblical counseling.
3. **Attend marriage-focused programs or counseling services offered by the church:**
   - Many churches offer marriage enrichment programs, workshops, or counseling services specifically tailored to help couples navigate challenges.
   - Take the initiative to participate in these programs and utilize the resources available.
   - Be open and honest about your struggles, and actively engage in the process of seeking growth and healing for your marriage.

Remember, seeking help through the church is an active step of faith and humility. It demonstrates a willingness to lean on God's guidance and the support of your church community. By taking these action steps, you can tap into the valuable resources and care available within the church to address and overcome the struggles in your marriage.

PRAYER FOR HELP

Heavenly Father, I humbly come before You, acknowledging my need for guidance and support in my marriage. I pray that You would lead me to the right biblical counselors who can provide wisdom and insight rooted in Your Word. Grant me humility, courage, and an open heart to receive the counsel and guidance You have prepared for me, that my marriage may be strengthened and restored according to Your perfect will. Amen.